Written By
Julie Carlyle-Hog

Illustrated By
Caner Soylu

For Cathie -
who has shown me all the love
and kindness in the world.

Published in association with Bear With Us Productions

Written By
Julie Carlyle-Hoggan

Illustrated By
Caner Soylu

They slept tucked behind a cobweb high in the dusty red brick fireplace of The Old School House on the bank of the River Thames.

A family of little elfins, with wings delicate as a butterfly's, flickering crystal rainbow light and scattering high birdsong giggles wherever they flew.

Each new day the Wingtip Elfins watched over the excited children in the classroom, helping them to grow with the strength of courage and confidence. They inspired in them the soft grace to take care of each other with patience and truth and love.

The eldest of the elfins was **Kitty Kindness.**

She glowed green as April's new leaves and scattered a fragrance as fresh as newly cut grass. Kitty was strong as an oak tree and her gift was kindness. As the children learnt to work and play together each day, she whispered tender words of friendliness, forgiveness and gentle reminders to think first of others.

Next came **Lennie Love.**

Shimmering red as the garden rose, Lennie had a heart as deep and wide as the river outside the window - flowing with love. Lennie's lesson was to teach care and compassion, the endless importance of loving and wanting the best for each other. Lennie shone cherry brightness across the classroom and warmed the children's fingers and toes with his cherishing ways.

Third in the elfin family was **Trinny Truth.**

She sparkled clear blue as a piece of turquoise glass rounded by the incoming tide of the sea. When Trinny was hovering nearby the children could faintly taste a soft sea-spray of delicate salt. With a fresh breeze, Trinny cut through their confusions and cries, with what was solid as the old school building itself - the importance of telling the truth.

And the smallest of them all, but so important to the children's lives... **Gilbert Giggle,**

who lit up the room with sunshine yellow and the golden sparkle of a simple chuckle. He melted away any worries or sadness with a moment's silliness and a soft wingtip's tickle. Gilbert was the children's favourite. His teaching was purely of fun, but no less important than the lessons of the other three.

The Wingtip Elfins had so much to teach these children, who loudly cried and freely laughed, openly showing their feelings. Although they couldn't be seen or heard by the grown-ups in the room, the children were alive to the guidance and giggles of these loving sprites.

On some days, at morning playtime, the children enjoyed the toys a little too much. Amy and Jess were the best of friends, but today they wanted to play with the same doll. They tussled and tugged at it from either side, their friendship lost in the angry upset of the moment.

"I had it first!" Amy cried.

Kitty Kindness and Trinny Truth fluttered gently down the chimney breast and hovered around them on the play-mat.

Kitty breathed gentle green patience across their frustrated tears. She sprinkled around them calming daydream images of happy games and shared smiles.

At the flicker of the elfins' wingtips, Amy and Jess took a pause and a moment's breath.

They both let go of the doll. Like a feather resting on the surface of the sea, Trinny landed lightly on Jess' shoulder. She began to ease the memory of which of them had first picked up the toy.

Remembering now the truth of how she had tried to snatch from Amy's hand, Jess delved into the toy-box and said,

"I'll play with this one instead!
The one with pink hair in a big frizz."

Amy grinned at her favourite friend, giggled happily and their game continued in peace and fun.

Suddenly, a shriek rang out. It was followed by another and a high-pitched wail.

"I want Mummy!" sobbed Ben.

He couldn't think of anything else but that. Lennie Love and Gilbert Giggle stirred from their chimney den and tripped across the room.

The elfin boys soothed their magic across Ben's crying eyes and reminded him of his mummy's big smile and the safety of her perfumed home-time hugs.

At the flicker of the elfins' wingtips, Ben took a pause and a moment's breath.

Lennie Love had reminded him, with a rosy glow of comfort and courage, that his mother always appeared in the doorway at the end of the afternoon.

"I'll see her later," Ben reassured himself and he relaxed.

Gilbert Giggle began to tickle his cheeks and he spun in a yellow blur before Ben's eyes, chasing and circling trying to nip his own wings, like a puppy chasing its tail on a sunny afternoon. Ben's spluttered cry became a chuckle and then, forgetting his worries, he laughed and squealed with delight.

Across the room, the art table was crowded with children, whose fingers were vibrant with paint splatters of the brightest colours. But there was trouble rising. One of the children was pointing at Joe's seaside picture and laughing,

"That's just a big splodgy mess!" Joe's tears dropped lightly and smudged the scene on the page.

Kitty Kindness and Lennie Love appeared softly overhead and blew a gentle woodland breeze of kind reassurance over Joe's hurt feelings.

They pointed out the beautiful colours he had used and reminded him how much he had been enjoying smearing the swirls of glooping paint.

At the flicker of the elfins' wingtips, Joe took a pause and a moment's breath.

Suddenly, Joe felt proud of his painting and smiled at its happy seaside memories. He cheerfully dabbed some more colour onto his brush and added a bright red beach ball to the scene.

Some time later, on the next table, Billy was staring at the worksheet in front of him. He recognised the images of a snake, an apple and a tree, but the letters printed alongside the pictures made no sense. Which one was S, which A and which T?

“Match the letter to the picture,” his soft-voiced teacher had asked.

Billy gripped his scribbly pencil and felt confused. The elfins were quick to realise, and Trinny Truth and Gilbert Giggle were soon hovering alongside him at the table. Trinny created in his mind a fresh blue-sky image of his teacher's kind face and encouraged Billy to simply tell the truth.

At the flicker of the elfins' wingtips, Billy took a pause and a moment's breath.

He called out to the teacher and asked for help, explaining timidly,

"I don't know how to do this."

The teacher sat alongside him to work through the letters. Together they practised them, until Billy clearly understood the different shapes and it was playtime again.

Gilbert Giggle whizzed amongst the sunbeams from end to end of the hall, as Billy chased him laughing. He let go of the worry of a tricky challenge and enjoyed this fun reward for his honesty and hard work.

After a while, when the little bell rang, it was time for the children to sit in a circle for singing. Charlie hated singing. He felt embarrassed and uncomfortable with such loudness ringing around the room.

Charlie hid himself, a small shape behind the bookshelf. The tears were streaming down his red cheeks, as he exhaled a tumble of "can'ts" and "won'ts."

"Everyone's looking at me!" he cried.

Sensing his fear, Lennie Love and Trinny Truth sailed swiftly into view. With a clear mirror's reflection, Trinny showed Charlie that, like so many other people, he was simply shy and feeling afraid. He needed to ask for a friend.

At the flicker of the elfins' wingtips, Charlie took a pause and a moment's breath.

Lennie planted the strength of deep red reassuring love in Charlie's heart. He encouraged Charlie to try singing with his voice, but also with a wide grin, so that the other children would see how much he was enjoying himself.

Charlie called out to a little girl nearby asking,
"Can I sit next to you, Kelsey?"

Bravely, he held onto her outstretched hand and joined the circle.

Very soon Charlie was lost in the music and the different voices around the room, as they rose into a blend of smiling song.

Now the day had come to an end.
The children left on their scooters and
bicycles for their tea-times at home.

Today, as yesterday and every day, the Wingtip Elfins had cast over the children their tiptoe lessons of love for each other and for themselves, of bravery and of truth.

Gilbert Giggle had sparkled nearby with sunlight tricks and tickles showing them the simple importance of everyday fun and laughter.

It was tiring work inspiring these beautiful children to become the best little people they could be. For now, in the quiet of the empty classroom, the elfins returned to their hidden corner in the chimney breast and, with a pause and a moment's breath, they tucked their weary wingtips behind the dusty cobweb and settled down for another starry night.

Printed in Great Britain
by Amazon